F-15 Eagle

In Action®

Written by David Doyle

Squadron Signal Publications

(Front Cover) A U.S Air Force F-15E Strike Eagle from the 366th Fighter Wing flies a mission over Iraq on 17 March 2016 in support of Operation Inherent Resolve, an international effort to help Iraqi Security Forces defeat ISIL. (Staff Sgt. Corey Hook/ USAF)

(Back Cover) The prototype Strike Eagle is carrying a load of 16 Mk. 82 500-pound bombs on the pylons and on racks attached to the conformal fuel tanks. To support heavy loads such as this, the landing gear and structure of the Strike Eagles would be strengthened. (National Museum of the United States Air Force)

About the In Action® Series

In Action® books, despite the title of the genre, are books that trace the development of a single type of aircraft, armored vehicle, or ship from prototype to the final production variant. Experimental or "one-off" variants can also be included. Our first *In Action*® book was printed in 1971.

ISBN 978-0-89747-839-7

Proudly printed in the U.S.A.
Copyright 2018 Squadron/Signal Publications
1115 Crowley Drive, Carrollton, TX 75006-1312 U.S.A.

Military/Combat Photographs and Snapshots

If you have any photos of aircraft, armor, soldiers, or ships of any nation, particularly wartime snapshots, please share them with us and help make Squadron/Signal's books all the more interesting and complete in the future. Any photograph sent to us will be copied and returned as requested. Electronic images are preferred. The donor will be fully credited for any photos used. Please send them to:

Squadron/Signal Publications
1115 Crowley Drive
Carrollton, TX 75006-1312 U.S.A.
www.Squadron.com

(Title Page) First flown in 1972, the McDonnell Douglas (later Boeing) F-15 Eagle was conceived as an absolute air superiority fighter, drawing on lessons learned in Vietnam. While within the USAF the aircraft has recently been eclipsed in the air superiority role by the F-22, the F-15E variant continues to serve admirably in the strike role.

Acknowledgments

As with all of my projects, this book would not have been possible without the generous help of many friends. Instrumental to the completion of this book were Tom Kailbourn, Dana Bell, Scott Taylor, the staff of the Still Pictures Unit of the National Archives, and Brett Stolle at the National Museum of the United States Air Force. My wonderful wife Denise not only scanned countless images for this and other efforts, but provides ongoing support and encouragement throughout these projects.

All photos not otherwise attributed are from the U.S. Department of Defense.

First flying in 1972, the McDonnell Douglas F-15 Eagle has transitioned from a true air superiority fighter into an all-weather strike aircraft Thus far, the aircraft has compiled one of the most enviable records of a post-Vietnam fighter, logging over 100 victories and no losses in air to air combat.

The bulk of the fighter aircraft operated by the USAF in Vietnam had been conceived during the Cold War as interceptors against nuclear-armed Soviet bombers. This strategy involved high-altitude, high-speed, air-to-air missile armament, and a long range. Utilizing these aircraft in Vietnam, with visual engagement rules, pointed to the shortcomings of the planning. Though both the F-105 and F-4 were deployed to Vietnam, neither were truly optimized for the role that they were forced into.

Further shortcomings of the then-current fighter strategy was revealed in July 1967 when the Soviets unveiled the MiG-25 Foxbat. The Foxbat was a twin-tail, twin-engine fighter aircraft capable of Mach 2.8. The US Air Force responded with renewed interest in what was then known as the F-X program. This program had begun as an effort to develop a multirole aircraft with variable geometry wings. After briefly considering a lightweight, single-engine fighter, a concept discarded in light of the shortcomings of the F-104, Project Definition Phase (PDP) contracts were issued to Fairchild-Republic, McDonnell Douglas, and North American Rockwell on December 30, 1968. After considering the proposals advanced by all three firms, a design and development contract was issued to McDonnell Douglas for the aircraft that would be designated F-15.

More than a year after the F-15A made its first flight, NASA conducted spin tests on a ⅜-scale remotely piloted research vehicle in the shape of an F-15. One of the three F-15 RPRVs is seen here being carried aloft from NASA Dryden on an NB-52. (National Museum of the United States Air Force)

The F-4 Phantom II was the USAF most successful fighter during the Vietnam war, but pointed to deficiencies in US strategy at the time in that it was not optimized for close air-to-air combat under visual engagement rules. Rather, instead the aircraft had been conceived to use missiles at long range, rather than guns in close range combat.

Development

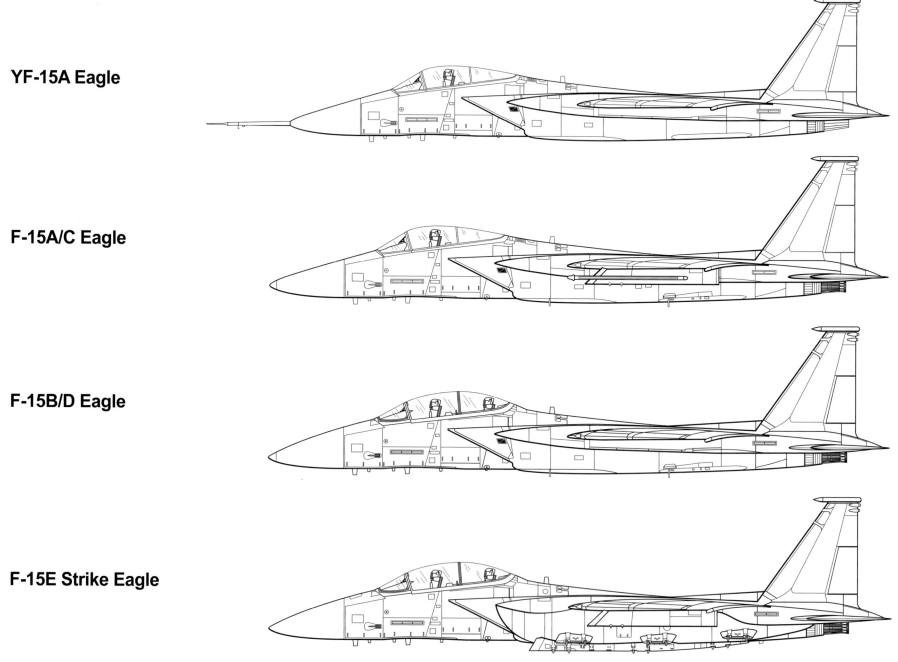

YF-15A Eagle

F-15A/C Eagle

F-15B/D Eagle

F-15E Strike Eagle

The first of the Eagles was F-15A USAF serial number 71-0280, one of 12 Category 1 (contractor development, test, and evaluation) F-15s that McDonnell Douglas produced. This plane is shown being rolled out of the St. Louis factory on 24 June 1972. (National Archives)

The first F-15A Eagle is viewed from a different perspective on the occasion of its official rollout on 24 June 1972. The F-15s were designed with provisions to mount two AIM-7 Sparrow missiles on each side of the fuselage, and mockups of these are present. (National Archives)

The first F-105A, 71-0280, appears here in a fairly fresh coat of paint, most likely Air Superiority Blue. Aside from stencils, the only markings are the national insignia, and "USAF" over "10280" on the vertical tail. The original, small speed brake is open. (National Museum of the United States Air Force)

After being rolled out in St. Louis, the first F-15A was partially disassembled and transported by C-5 Galaxy transport to Edwards Air Force Base for testing. The plane is shown here after arriving at Edwards on 11 July 1972, 16 days before its first flight. (National Archives)

The first Eagle, YF-15A USAF serial number 71-0280, is shown in its early Air Superiority Blue paint job with Day-Glo orange trim. By the time this photo was taken, the intense sun of Edwards Air Force Base evidently had faded the orange to yellow. (National Museum of the United States Air Force)

Procurement of the F-15 was such that no "XF-15" aircraft were built. Rather, the aircraft went from drawing board to production, with the first 18 examples being Full Scale Development (FSD) aircraft. The first 10 single seat aircraft, serial numbers 71-0280 through 71-0289, were considered Category I test aircraft (as were two two-seat TF-15A aircraft, serial numbers 71-290 and 71-291), while the next eight aircraft, serial numbers 72-0113 through 72-0120), were considered Category II test aircraft. These initial production aircraft have been identified variously as F-15 FSD, YF-15A, F-15, and Cat I aircraft. In this volume, we use the YF-15A term for clarity.

The first of the aircraft, serial number 71-0280, rolled out of McDonnell Douglas's St. Louis plant on 26 June, 1972. Owing in part to the urban nature of the St. Louis plant, aircraft was subsequently dismantled and flown in the belly of a C-5 Galaxy to Edwards Air Force Base, California, where it was reassembled for its first flight. That flight occurred on 27 July, 1972, with McDonnell Douglas chief test pilot Irving Burrows at the controls.

Powered by Pratt & Whitney F100 engines, providing a thrust to weight ratio greater than 1:1, the first flight was without hitch, but for a minor problem with a landing gear door. During the first flight, altitude was limited to 12,000 feet and a speed of 250 knots. Subsequent flights gave a fuller appreciation of the type's capabilities. By late October 1973, eleven of the test aircraft were flying, and altitudes of 60,000 feet and speeds of Mach 2.3 had been reached. Few problems had been discovered, those being confined to buffeting, which was corrected by the removal of a diagonal area from the wing tip, and the necessity of increasing the area of the airbrake substantially.

An early YF-15A test plane is armed with cluster bombs and AIM-7 and AIM-9 missiles. On the nose is an air-data boom, with sensors for monitoring angle of attack, angle of sideslip, static pressure, total pressure, outside air temperature, and total air temperature. (National Museum of the United States Air Force)

YF-15A 71-0280 was painted overall in Air Superiority Blue, with areas of Day-Glo Orange. Marked on each side of the nose and the vertical tails were a stylized F-15 silhouette and the McDonnell Douglas logo. "EAGLE" also was marked on the nose. (National Museum of the United States Air Force)

Details of the layout of the Day-Glo orange paint on the first YF-15A, serial number 71-0280, are apparent on this view from below during flight. Initially, the first YF-15As had squared wingtips and straight leading edges on the horizontal stabilizers. (National Museum of the United States Air Force)

YF-15A USAF serial number 71-0280 is viewed from the left side during an early test flight, showing the Day-Glow orange areas on the vertical tail, the horizontal stabilizer, the side of the engine intakes, the wing, and the air-data boom. (National Museum of the United States Air Force)

The first YF-15A is viewed from the upper right, providing more details of the Day-Glow orange areas. A close inspection of these photos of YF-15A 71-0280 reveal that the Day-Glow paint was not applied to the leading edges of the wings, fins, and stabilizers. (National Museum of the United States Air Force)

An early, test-model YF-15A is flying in formation below a Boeing KC-97 Stratofreighter during an aerial refueling exercise in September 1974. The YF-15As and subsequent models had an air-refueling receptacle on the top of the left wing near the wing root. (National Museum of the United States Air Force)

YF-15A-4-MC serial number 71-0287 approaches Boeing KC-135A-BN Stratotanker serial number 55-3135 for refueling. This Eagle first flew on 25 August 1973, and was employed in spin-recovery and angle-of-attack trials and in fuel-system testing. (National Museum of the United States Air Force)

During a test flight, McDonnell Douglas YF-15A-3-MC serial number 71-0286 is carrying Mk. 82 500-pound bombs on multiple-ejector racks. This Eagle was assigned to the combined McDonnell Douglas/U.S. Air Force F-15 Joint Test Force at Edwards Air Force Base, California, from September 1973 to November 1980, where it was used as a test aircraft for armament development and external fuel stores. By the 1990s it was displayed at the Octave Chanute Aerospace Museum, Rantoul, Illinois, and it later found a new home at the Saint Louis Science Center. (National Museum of the United States Air Force)

YF-15A serial number 71-0287 makes a landing approach with its dive brake extended; the spin-chute container is visible between the engine nozzles, painted in day-glo orange and black-and-white checkers. A large dive brake has replaced the original, smaller one. (National Museum of the United States Air Force)

The first YF-15A is parked at the McDonnell Douglas plant in St. Louis, Missouri. No Day-Glo paint panels are now absent. After serving as a test plane, YF-15A 71-0280 had a second career, traveling around the United States as a static-display recruiting tool for the Air Force.

The 13th preproduction YF-15A, USAF serial number 72-0115, was used for operational testing. Here, it is loaded with blue and Olive Drab practice bombs and inert AIM-9L Sidewinder missiles. Orange-colored pylons at various points hold orange cameras for documenting the test-firing of the plane's air-to-air missiles. Placed at intervals on the wings and the fuselage are black-and-white photo-reference markings. Numerous photo-reference markings are also on the bomb pylons. (National Museum of the United States

Wingtip Development

YF-15

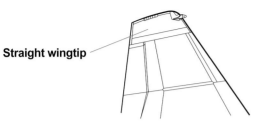

Straight wingtip

F-15A

Raked wingtip with 4 square feet (0.4 square meters) removed from prototype wingtip

Elevon Development

YF-15

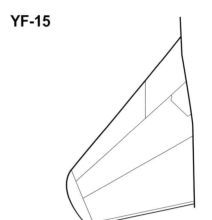

F-15A

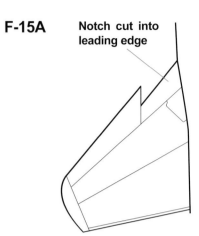

Notch cut into leading edge

During flight testing of the YF-15A, wing-buffeting was encountered; the fix was to rake the wingtip. Further, after the first three YF-15A test planes experienced flutter, the straight leading edges of the stabilators received a notched, "dog-tooth" design.

The YF-15A and subsequent models of the Eagle have separate, articulated intakes for the two engines. These are located to the sides of the cockpit, as seen in a photo of the first YF-15A. This plane lacked the production F-15s' M61 cannon in the right wing root. (National Museum of the United States Air Force)

In this photo of the first YF-15A, the Day-Glo orange areas on the upper surfaces are still quite fresh; later, these areas became faded where they were exposed directly to the sun. This YF-15A was used for envelope exploration, testing handling, and external stores. (National Museum of the United States Air Force)

The instrument panel in the cockpit of a YF-15A at Edwards Air Force Base on 20 March 1975 varied considerably from the Category 1 preproduction YF-15As. At the upper center of the instrument panel are communications and heads-up-display controls. (National Archives)

The left console of a YF-15A under evaluation at Edwards Air Force Base is seen on 20 March 1975. The console included communications controls and the throttle lever, on which were switches for systems such as the speed brakes and rudder trim. (National Archives)

The cockpit of a YF-15A is viewed from a slightly different perspective in an April 1975 photo. At the bottom center is the control stick, on the grip of which were auto-pilot, weapons, trim, nose-gear, trigger, air-fueling release, and weapons-release switches. (National Archives)

The right console of the YF-15A includes the oxygen regulator, control panels for the engine, navigation, compass, environmental control system, lights, and the tactical electronic warfare system (TEWS). In the foreground is the Escapac IC-7 ejection seat. (National Archives)

13

Following McDonnell Douglas's and the Air Force's successful testing of the preproduction YF-15As, full production of the single-seat F-15As and the two-seat F-15Bs began at McDonnell Douglas's St. Louis plant. A total of 384 F-15As were completed. Shown here is F-15A-11-MC USAF serial number 74-0100, one of 18 planes completed in the -11 production block. There were consecutively numbered production blocks for the F-15A from 1 to 20. The "MC" suffix pertains to McDonnell Douglas. The "FF" tail code represented the 1st Tactical Fighter Wing. (National Museum of the United States Air Force)

Delivery of Eagles to operational USAF units began in November 1974, with deliveries to the 555th Tactical Fighter Training Squadron of the 58th Tactical Training Wing at Luke AFB, Arizona. In January 1976 F-15A aircraft were delivered to the 1st Tactical Fighter Wing at Langley Air Force Base, Virginia, marking the initial delivery to a combat wing.

Once fielded, problems began to surface with the F100 engines. Redesign of some components as well as changes to the maintenance cycle resolved these problems, however, a less-serious engine problem was introduced. That was a shortage of engines, a result of the aforementioned issues coupled with strikes at component manufacturers, which led to McDonnell Douglas delivering and the Air Force accepting aircraft without engines.

The F-15s went next on strength with the 32nd Tactical Fighter Squadron, which was under control of the Dutch Air Force while fulfilling its NATO mission. Also equipped with the Eagle was the 33rd Tactical Fighter Wing at Eglin Air Force Base. A few interceptor squadrons attached to the Tactical Air Command exchanged their F-106 Delta Darts for the new McDonnell fighter as well.

By 1982 the F-15A (and B) was beginning to show its age. A Multi-Stage Improvement Program (MSIP) was developed which would significantly improve the aircraft. However, this project was subsequently cancelled, citing cost. Instead, the aircraft were given more modest upgrade utilizing a portion of a similar program developed for the F-15C/D.

The dual-engine F-15A poses next to its smaller, single-engine stable mate in the USAF air-superiority-fighter inventory, the General Dynamics F-16 Fighting Falcon. The F-15A entered operational service in November 1974, almost four years before the F-16. (National Museum of the United States Air Force)

There were many access panels and doors on the F-15A to allow ground crews and technicians to work on the complex interior systems of the plane. Those doors and panels have been removed or swung open in this photograph. At the front is the open radome for the Hughes AN/APG-63 radar. The two upward-opening doors to the rear of the radar antenna housed radar electronics boxes. Those doors themselves held the pitot tubes and contained the forward antennas for the AN/ALQ-128 Electronic Warfare Warning Set.

F-15A-15-MC USAF serial number 76-0043 is seen from the upper right front with its access doors open and access panels removed. The doors along the front of the fuselage had recessed latch handles. In the right wing root is the one gun installed in the F-15A: the M61A1 Vulcan 20mm gun, a rotary, six-barreled, Gatling-type, cannon with a rate of fire of 4,000 or 6,000 rounds per minute. The speed brake, which on production F-15s has approximately 50-percent more area than those of the preproduction F-15s, is extended. (National Museum of the United States Air Force)

The radome of the F-15A, seen here open, comprised a synthetic-foam core within an inner and outer skin. The radome was able to withstand temperatures up to 500 degrees Fahrenheit. "RADIATION HAZARD" is painted on the front of the radar antenna.

With the radome and the access doors open, the antenna of the Hughes AN/APG-63 radar is visible to the left. To the rear of it are bays containing electronics for the radar, such as the power supply, wave-guide assemblies, radar transmitter, and data processor.

The antenna of the AN/APG-63 radar is viewed from the front, with the radome swung to the right side. A strut at the bottom of the radome locks it into the open position, and a strut is also used to hold the radar electronics-bay door in the open position.

17

This view from below of an F-15A in flight provides a clear idea of the shape of the raked wingtips and the notched leading edges of the stabilators. On the centerline pylon is a 610-gallon auxiliary fuel tank. The titanium skin around the rears of the engines was left unpainted. The fuselage extensions to the outboard sides of the engine nozzles also were bare metal except for the rear tips. (National Museum of the United States Air Force)

With sheaves of checklists and manuals in hand, an F-15A pilot stands poised at the bottom of the boarding ladder for the cockpit in this undated photograph. The national insignia used at the time, partially visible behind the boarding ladder, featured a blue circle with white star and red and white bars to the sides, with no blue borders around the bars. The number 7118 is stenciled in black vertically on the nose-gear door. (National Museum of the United States Air Force)

An F-15A undergoes climactic testing in a simulated tropical environment in a hangar at McKinley Climatic Laboratory, Eglin Air Force Base, Florida, in 1975. A flexible hose from the test cart is plugged into the ground-cooling receptacle on the fuselage. (National Museum of the United States Air Force)

The same F-15A depicted in the preceding photo is towed out of the McKinley Climatic Laboratory following a two-month period of climatic tests to establish the plane's ability to withstand extremes of atmospheric conditions. (National Museum of the United States Air Force)

Eagle prototypes and early F-15As and F-15Bs had the Douglas IC-7 Escapac ejection seat. Escapac seats were later replaced by the McDonnell Douglas ACES II ejection seat. A key difference between these types was that the Escapac had a pull ring at the center front of the seat cushion to eject the seat, while the ACES II had a pull ring on each side.

This view of technicians aligning the heads-up display (HUD) around August 1973 offers a good view of the top of the fuselage and wings aft of the cockpit. The speed brake is the original design, found on preproduction and very-early F-15As. (National Museum of the United States Air Force)

Escapac IC-7

McDonnell Douglas ACES II

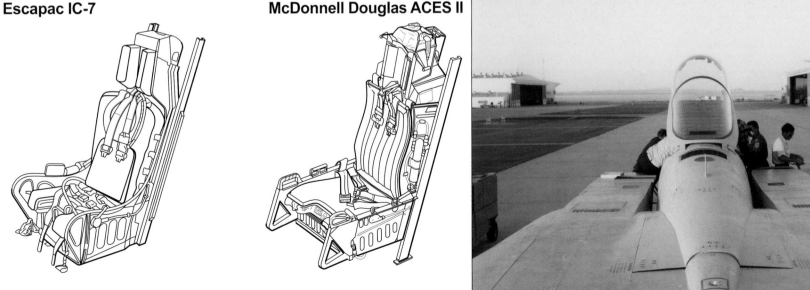

Among the 12 Category 1 preproduction F-15s was a pair of two-seater F-15B, USAF serial numbers 71-0290 and, seen here, 71-0291. Originally designated TF-15A, the F-15B was intended as a training aircraft, with flight controls in the rear cockpit. (National Museum of the United States Air Force)

The F-15B was initially designated the TF-15. The aircraft was the two-seat training version of the Eagle. With the same overall dimensions as the F-15A, the F-15B differed chiefly by having a larger canopy enclosing a second seat. In order to make room for the second seat, the fuel tank size was reduced slightly and the Internal Countermeasure Set (ICS) was not installed. No changes were made to the armament, and the performance of the aircraft was essentially the same as that of the F-15A.

The first flight of an F-15B, then designated TF-15A, was made by serial number 71-0290 on 18 October 1973. One TF-15A was built for every 6 F-15A aircraft. The first TF-15A delivery to an operational USAF unit occurred on 4 November 1974, when serial number 73-0108 was turned over to the 555th Tactical Fighter Training Squadron of the 58th Tactical Training Wing at Luke AFB, Arizona. President Gerald Ford was the keynote speaker for the occasion.

Following the initial test program, the first two TF-15A aircraft, serial numbers 71-0290 and 71-0291, were later modified for use in further development of the Eagle. Aircraft 71-0290 was modified for use as part of the Short Take Off and Landing (STOL) program and the Maneuver Technology Demonstrator (Agile Eagle) program. The second aircraft was used in the evaluation of the FAST Pack conformal fuel tanks and LANTIRN pod prior to becoming the development aircraft for the F-15E Strike Eagle. Other F-15B aircraft produced were 73-108 through 73-114, 74-137 through 74-142, 75-080 through 75-089, 76-124 through 76-142 and 77-154 through 77-168. Serial numbers 76-1524 and 76-1525 were delivered to the Israeli Air Force.

The F-15B featured a new canopy that was slightly enlarged at the rear to accommodate the rear seat. The second F-15B, again shown here, had markings for "F-15," a silhouette of the plane, and the McDonnell Douglas logo on the nose and the vertical tails. (National Museum of the United States Air Force)

An F-15B is lining up for an aerial refueling. The plane is painted in overall Air Superiority Blue, which was used on the earliest F-15s. Later, this F-15B would receive a red, white, and blue scheme similar to one intended for the USAF Thunderbirds. (National Museum of the United States Air Force)

The F-15C improved upon the F-15A in several respects. The F-15C carried 280 more gallons internally, had provisions for mounting conformal fuel tanks, and featured improved Electronic Counter Measures (ECM) equipment and a stronger airframe. The Escapac IC-7 ejection seat of the preproduction and early F-15A/B had been replaced following Block 16 by the ACES II ejection seat. After F-15C production commenced, further improvements were made to the plane. The F-15C first flew on 26 February 1979. This photo shows the first of the C-model Eagles, F-15C-21-MC 78-0468, with "F-15C," the McDonnell Douglas logo, and "NO. 1" marked on the nose. (National Museum of the United States Air Force)

The introduction of the F-15C, first flown on 26 February 1979, lessened the amount of maintenance required by deletion of the trouble-prone "turkey feathers" that covered the variable exhaust nozzles of the engines on the F-15A from the onset of production. These were also removed from the F-15As in the field. Compared to its predecessor, the electronics suite of the F-15C showed several improvements, most notably a Programmable Signal Processor which allowed for rapid switching of the radar between modes.

The F-15C also introduced the "FAST" (Fuel and Sensor Tactical) packs to the airframe. Attached to the fuselage outside each air intake, these tanks conform to the aerodynamic shape of the fuselage, increasing fuel capacity with little change in aircraft performance. Now known as Conformal Fuel Tanks (CFT), these tanks, though rarely removed, can be removed by ground crews in about 15 minutes. The tanks have a capacity of 849 gallons, although by reducing the amount of fuel equipment such as cameras, radar jammers, laser designators and infrared equipment can be carried.

A further increase in range was achieved by the addition of internal wing leading and trailing edge fuel tanks, as well as additional tankage inside the fuselage. The internal fuel capacity of the F-15C is 2,070 gallons, which could be augmented by the FAST packs as well as three external drop tanks. The extra fuel meant that the F-15C had a considerably higher gross weight than the F-15A, requiring redesigned landing gear and tires, changes that are noticeable to the observer. A total of 408 F-15Cs were delivered to the USAF, with additional examples going to Saudi Arabia.

F-15C-21-MC serial number 78-0468 is viewed from the upper right during a test flight. The F-15s followed a serial production-block numbering system from model to model: the -21 suffix for the first block of F-15Cs followed the -20 block number of the previous batch of F-15Bs. (National Museum of the United States Air Force)

F-15C-24-MC USAF serial number 79-0015 is carrying a full complement of four AIM-7 Sparrow air-to-air, radar-homing missiles on the fuselage and four AIM-9 Sidewinder short-range air-to-air missiles on launcher rails on the pylons. A 610-gallon auxiliary fuel tank is on the centerline hardpoints. The "CR" tail code represents the 32nd Tactical Fighter Squadron. (National Museum of the United States Air Force)

An F-15C is viewed from the front, with conformal fuel tanks on carts to the sides, in an April 1983 photograph. Originally known as FAST (Fuel And Sensor Tactical) tanks but now called conformal fuel tanks (CFTs), they could be attached to or removed from the sides of the fuselage as the mission dictated. Each tank added 849 U.S. gallons of fuel to the F-15C's total capacity. Pylons were built into the CFTs to accept bombs or AIM-7 Sparrows. (National Museum of the United States Air Force)

The first F-15C, 79-0468, undergoes a test flight, armed with AIM-7 sparrow missiles. Visible below the rear of the fuselage are two orange-colored cameras and mounts for documenting the test-firing of the air-to-air missiles. (National Museum of the United States Air Force)

F-15C number 1, USAF serial number 79-0468, banks over hilly desert terrain. Sparrow missiles are mounted, but test cameras are not present during this mission. The variable-geometry air intakes, which operated automatically, are canted downward. (National Museum of the United States Air Force)

The lines of the F-15C, which entered production in 1978, were essentially the same as for the F-15A. Most of the differences were in improved systems, including strengthened landing gear, a new digital central computer, provisions for conformal fuel tanks, and the new APG-63 radar, with a revolutionary, new programmable signal processor that, among other things, allowed for progressive upgrades in the weapons suite.

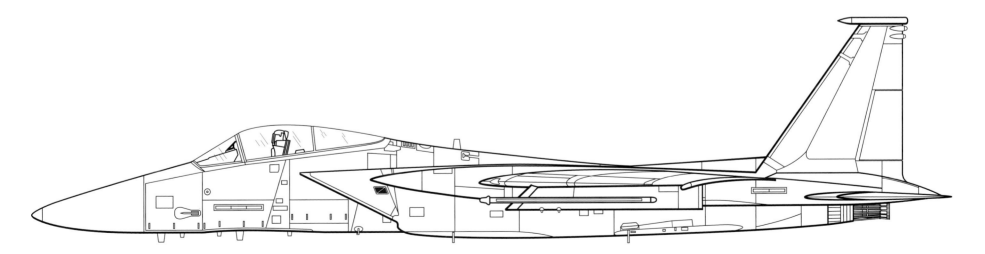

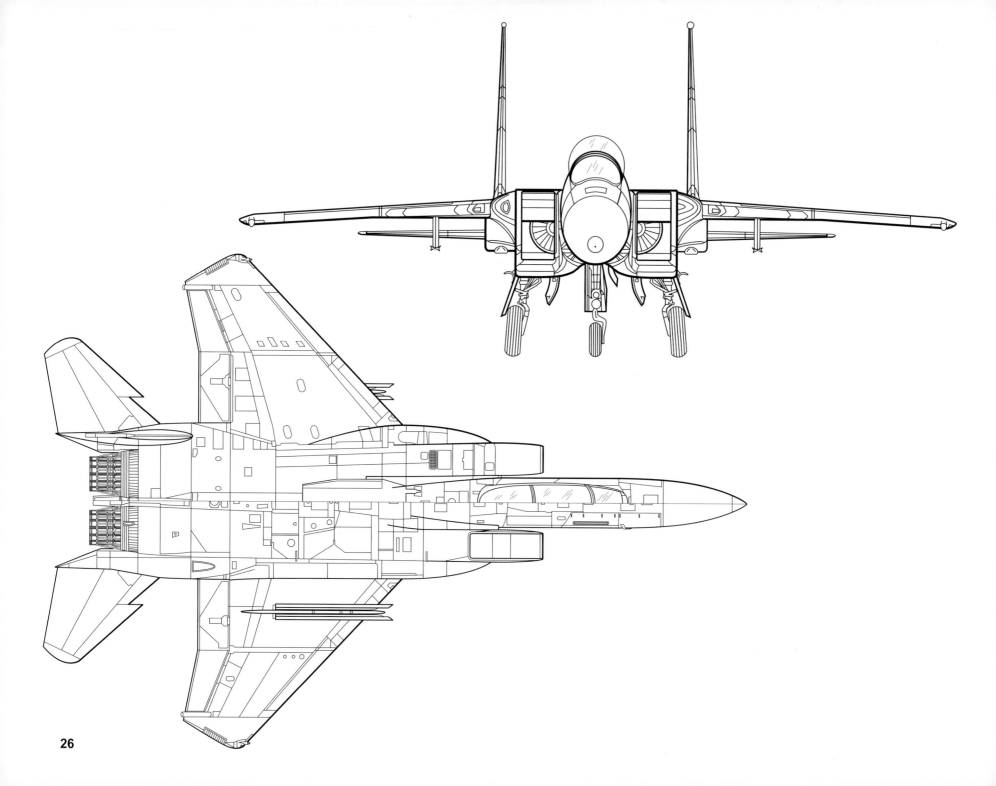

As the F-15A has a two-seat version, the F-15B, the F-15C's two-seat version is the F-15D. The U.S. Air Force received 61 of them, and 36 were distributed to Israel, Japan, and Saudi Arabia. This example, F-15D-25-MC USAF serial number 79-009, bears tail markings for the 54th Fighter Squadron (yellow stripe), 3rd Wing ("AK"), Eleventh Air Force, based at Elmendorf Air Force Base, Alaska. On the inside of the left vertical tail is a representation of the Big Dipper and the North Star. (Dana Bell)

The F-15D was created to serve as the two-seat trainer version of the F-15C. As such, it featured all the improvements incorporated into the F-15C airframe, albeit with reduced internal fuel capacity. The two-place cockpit is shown to good advantage in this photo of NASA F-15D 897, taken on 10 November 2015. (NASA)

McDonnell Douglas F-15D-34-MC 82-046 of the 27th Tactical Fighter Squadron (yellow tail band), 1st Tactical Air Wing ("FF" tail code), is parked in a revetment while based in Saudi Arabia around early 1991. AIM-9 Sidewinders are mounted on the pylons.

F-15D-36-MC 83-050 of the 27th Tactical Fighter Squadron, 1st Tactical Fighter Wing, is parked next to another F-15 at a desert base in March 1991. On the side of the engine air inlet trunk is the insignia of the 1st TFW. The number 3050 is marked just aft of the radome. (Dana Bell)

Under the project name Strike Eagle, McDonnell Douglas and Hughes Aircraft undertook a joint, self-funded project in the late 1970s to convert the second F-15B, 71-0291, to a multi-role Eagle specializing in ground-attack, supplanting the aging F-111. Strike Eagle was equipped with conformal fuel tanks; a new radar, the AN/APG-70, with air-to-ground and air-to-air functions; and a rear cockpit outfitted for a weapons system operator (WSO). This plane, shown here, made its first flight on 8 July 1980 and became the basis of the F-15E Strike Eagle. (National Museum of the United States Air Force)

Cathode-ray tubes (CRTs) were a key element of the front and rear cockpits of the F-15E, providing various imaging aids. The CRTs are lit up in this demonstrator, with the WSO's displays appearing in the foreground, at the bottom of the photo, and the pilot's CRTs and windshield appearing higher up. The cathode-ray tube displays in the F-15E Strike Eagle offer many benefits to the crew, including improved navigational abilities, more accurate and effective weapons delivery, and overall better systems operations. The pilot has at his disposal redesigned controls, a heads-up display featuring wide field of vision, and three cathode-ray tubes, which offer multi-purpose displays for navigation, systems operations, and weapons delivery. The weapons system officer in the rear seat has an improved ALQ-135 electronic warfare system with broadband jammer, as well as four CRT displays for weapons selection, radar, and monitoring of enemy tracking systems.

In an overhead view of Strike Eagle 71-0291, white visual-reference markings are around the air refueling receptacle. The dark gray paint of the camouflage scheme was nearly equal in tone to the dark green, so it is sometimes difficult to distinguish the two colors. Low-visibility black national insignia were applied to the left wing top and to the sides of the fuselage to the front of the engine intakes. This Eagle had been used as a development aircraft for the FAST pack conformal fuel tanks. Following its first flight, serial number 71-0291 flew on a demonstration tour in Europe and made an appearance at the Farnborough Air show in September 1980. The plane was the winning entry in the competition with the F-16XL for the Enhanced Tactical Fighter (ETF) to replace the F-111, and was employed in tests for that purpose at Edwards Air Force Base, California, and Eglin Air Force Base, Florida. This aircraft currently is on display at the Royal Saudi Air Force Museum in Riyadh. (National Museum of the United States Air Force)

Strike Eagle 71-0291 is viewed from the rear in a photograph taken in July 1980. "Turkey feathers," long, thin, vanes around the engine exhausts, are present on these engines; they enhanced engine performance but, as high-maintenance items, they often were removed. (National Museum of the United States Air Force)

Initially, Strike Eagle 71-0291 had the Compass Ghost camouflage scheme. Later, it was repainted in a three-color wrap-around camouflage scheme (sometimes disparagingly called "slime green"), comprising dark gray and two shades of green. (National Museum of the United States Air Force)

The first production Strike Eagle, F-15E-41-MC 86-183, is undergoing a test flight. The production F-15s feature two LANTIRN (low-altitude navigation targeting infrared for night) pods under the engine intakes. These combined terrain-following radar and forward-looking radar to give the pilot and the WSO exceptional navigating and targeting aids. Dummy LANTIRN pods were mounted on this plane. The real pods, which became operational in 1987, consisted of the AAQ-13 Navigation Pod on the right pylon and the AAQ-14 Target Pod on the left pylon. (National Museum of the United States Air Force)

The first production F-15E demonstrates its remarkable climbing ability during a test flight over a desert in September 1987. The production F-15Es were painted overall in a dark shade of gray, Gunship Gray (FS36118). The titanium skin around the aft parts of the jet engines remained unpainted. Hardpoints for two air-to-air missiles are on the lower part of each conformal fuel tank. (National Museum of the United States Air Force)

An F-15E Strike Eagle is viewed from directly below during a flight in February 1987. It is carrying three drop tanks as well as the two LANTIRN pods under the engine intakes. Since the LANTIRN pods only became operational during 1987, the two seen here may have been dummies. The longer pod on the left station represents the AAQ-14 Target Pod, while the shorter pod represents the AAQ-13 Navigation Pod. (National Museum of the United States Air Force)

A ground crewman assists the pilot of an F-15A that has arrived at Luke Air Force Base, Arizona, in May 1974. This was several months before the first operational F-15 was delivered to Luke, in November 1974. Two more F-15As are in the background. (National Archives)

An F-15A, USAF serial number 72-0115, poses next to one of its ancestors, a Spad XIII fighter from World War I, at Lockbourne Air Force Base, Ohio, on the occasion of that base's renaming to Rickenbacker Air Force Base, 17 May 1974. (National Archives)

F-15 Specifications

Specifications			
	F-15A	F-15C	F-15E
DIMENSIONS	feet-inches	feet-inches	feet-inches
Wingspan	42'9.75"	42'9.75"	42'9.75"
Length	63'9"	63'9"	63'9"
Height	18'5.5"	18'5.5"	18'5.5"
FUEL	pounds	pounds	gallons
Integral	11,908	13,771	13,432
External (Max)	23,803	36,200	36,200
In-Flight Refueling	yes	yes	yes
WEIGHTS	lbs	lbs	lbs
Empty Weight	28,600	28,600	31,700
Maximum Gross Weight	68,000	68,000	81,000
PERFORMANCE			
Maximum Speed	1,650 mph @36,000 ft	1,650 mph @36,000 ft	1,650 mph @40,000 ft
Service Ceiling	60,000 feet	60,000 feet	60,000 feet
Range, w/external tanks	2,878 miles	2,878 miles	2,878 miles
Range, w/conformal tanks	N/A	3,450 miles	3,570 miles
ENGINES			
Type	2 x Pratt & Whitney F-100-PW-100	2 x Pratt & Whitney F-100-PW-220	2 x Pratt & Whitney F-100-PW-229
Maximum Thrust	23,450 lbs each	23,450 lbs each	29,000 lbs each
COST	$27.9 million each	$29.9 million each	$31.1 million each
ARMAMENT			
Cannon	1 x M61A1 20mm Vulcan	1 x M61A1 20mm Vulcan	1 x M61A1 20mm Vulcan
Ammunition	940 rounds	940 rounds	940 rounds
Missile	4 x AIM-9 Sidewinder, up to four AIM-7 Sparrow or AIM-120 AMRAAM	4 x AIM-9 Sidewinder, up to four AIM-7 Sparrow or AIM-120 AMRAAM	4 x AIM-9 Sidewinder, up to four AIM-7 Sparrow or 8 AIM-120 AMRAAM

"Streak Eagle," preproduction F-15A 72-0119, was diverted from the test program to serve as a vehicle for attempting a new time-to-climb record in 1975. This plane served in that role in an unpainted state to reduce its weight; "Streak Eagle" art was on the nose. (National Museum of the United States Air Force)

"Streak Eagle" set eight new time-to-climb world records between 16 January and 1 February 1975, ultimately climbing to 98,425 feet in 3.5 minutes from brake release at takeoff. Suited up next to the plane is one of its pilots, Maj. Dave Peterson, USAF. (National Museum of the United States Air Force)

"Streak Eagle" flies over downtown St. Louis, Missouri. The patchy, multicolored appearance of the plane was owing to the unpainted mix of composites and metals used on the aircraft. "USAF" over "20119" were marked in black on the vertical tail. (National Museum of the United States Air Force)

The air intake of "Streak Eagle" is canted downward in this shot, revealing a wedge-shaped area of metal skin that is lighter than the surrounding surfaces. Under the canopy to the rear of the pilot's seat is a white object that was unique to the "Streak Eagle": a large VHF antenna. (National Museum of the United States Air Force)

"Streak Eagle" was equipped with an air-data boom with alpha and beta vanes. (Alpha vanes register angle of attack, while beta vanes detect aircraft angle of sideslip.) By not painting "Streak Eagle," the plane was spared 50 pounds of extra weight. Equipment not essential to the mission was removed, such as the gun and ammunition, radar and fire-control gear, flap and speed-brake actuators, and nonessential communications devices. (National Museum of the United States Air Force)

By the time this photograph of "Streak Eagle" was taken, a large insignia had been applied to the vertical tail. Its motto read "Aquila Maxima," Latin for "Greatest Eagle." Visible on the insignia is an eagle's head with a red, white, and blue streamer behind it. (National Museum of the United States Air Force)

The "Aquila Maxima" insignia on the left vertical tail of the "Streak Eagle" is partially visible. "Streak Eagle" currently is in storage at the National Museum of the United States Air Force, at Wright-Patterson Air Force Base. (National Museum of the United States Air Force)

F-15A-6-MC 72-117 was one of the Category 2 preproduction Eagles, and it is seen in its original Air Superiority Blue camouflage, banking right over Locks & Dam 27 near St. Louis. This was one of the F-15As transferred to the Israeli Defense Forces/Air Force. (National Archives)

On 20 March 1976, F-15A-10-MC 74-083, the first Eagle to be delivered to the 1st Tactical Fighter Wing, is parked next to a General Dynamics F-111. The nickname "Peninsula Patriot" is written in small, old-fashioned lettering aft of the radome. (National Museum of the United States Air Force)

Photographed on 20 March 1976, McDonnell Douglas F-15B-10-MC USAF serial number 74-137 bears the "FF" tail code of the 1st Tactical Fighter Wing. The last three digits of the serial number, 137, are stenciled on the fuselage just aft of the radome. (National Museum of the United States Air Force)

F-15A-9-MC 73-100 was not yet assigned unit markings when this photo was taken. This was the first F-15 to leave the factory painted in the Compass Ghost camouflage, which featured patterns of Dark Ghost Gray (FS36320) over Light Ghost Gray (FS36375). (National Archives)

F-15s are undergoing depot maintenance at Warner Robbins Air Logistics Center at Robbins Air Force Base, Georgia, in November 1977. Those for which tail markings are visible are, left to right, F-15A-9-MC 73-0098, 405th Tactical Training Wing; F-15A-11-MC 74-0107, 1st Fighter Wing; and 73-3102, which is probably an error on the painters part, and should likely be instead 73-0102. (National Museum of the United States Air Force)

Carrying a 610-gallon auxiliary fuel tank on the centerline, F-15A-15-MC 76-0039 of the 36th Tactical Fighter Wing, stationed at Bitburg Air Base, Federal Republic of Germany, visits RAF Alconbury, England, for aggressor training exercises in October 1977. (National Museum of the United States Air Force)

Four of the U.S. Air Force's fighter jets are lined up during a tactical-fighter training mission out of Luke Air Force Base on 1 August 1979. At the top is F-15A-16-MC 76-0078 of the 550th Tactical Training Squadron, 58th Tactical Training Wing. Below the F-15A are an F-4C Phantom II, an F-104 Starfighter, and an F-5E Tiger II.

On 20 March 1978, F-15B-16-MV 76-0135 of the 7th Tactical Fighter Squadron, 49th Tactical Fighter Wing, is parked on a hardstand at Holloman Air Force Base, New Mexico. The 49th TFW's original insignia is on the engine intake trunk. (National Museum of the United States Air Force)

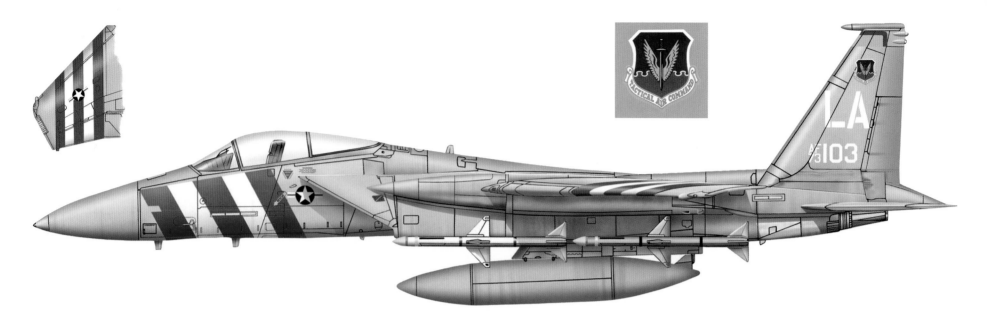

McDonnell Douglas F-15A-9-MC Eagle serial number 73-0103, was painted in Air Superiority Blue, with red and white stripes painted on the wings and forward fuselage for high visibility, while serving with the 461st Tactical Fighter Training Squadron, 405th Tactical Fighter Training Wing, at Luke Air Force Base, Arizona, in the last half of the 1970s.

Based at Langley Air Force Base, Virginia, F-15A-17-MC serial number 76-0100 served with the 48th Fighter Interceptor Squadron in the 1980s. This squadron was equipped with F-15As from 1982 to 1991, during which year the squadron was inactivated. The insignia of the 48th FIS is on the side of the engine intake.

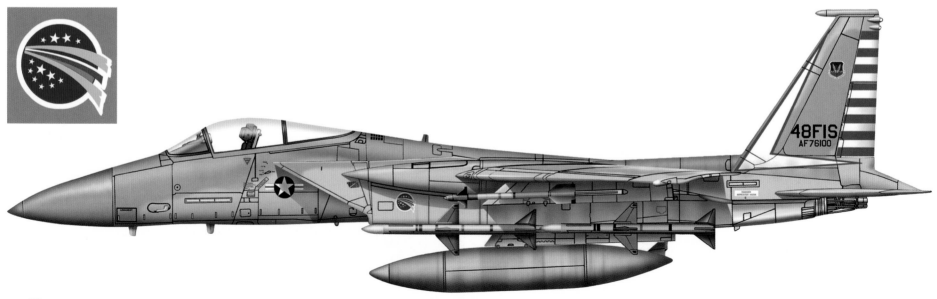

Two 49th Fighter Wing F-15s are sitting on a hardstand awash with recent rainwater at Holloman Air Force Base, New Mexico, in May 1980. Both Eagles have red bands on the upper parts of their vertical tails, indicating they belonged to the 9th Fighter Squadron. (National Museum of the United States Air Force)

In a companion view to the preceding photo, two of the 9th Fighter Squadron's F-15A-18-MCs, serial numbers 77-0069, left, and 77-0073, right, prepare to taxi out on a mission at Holloman Air Force Base, New Mexico, on 1 May 1980.

Two F-15 Eagles of the 433rd Fighter Weapons Squadron have completed a training mission and are homeward bound to Nellis Air Force Base, Nevada, on 1 May 1980. An AIM-9L Sidewinder air-to-air missile is mounted a launching rail on the outboard side of the left pylon on each aircraft. On the inboard side of the left pylons are combat training system pods, apparently of the P3 or P4 type produced by Cubic Corp.

41

Speed brake extended, F-15A-18-MC 76-0119 of the 433rd Fighter Weapons Squadron, 57th Wing, comes in for a landing at Nellis Air Force Base, Nevada, on 1 May 1980. On the tops of the vertical tails were black-and-yellow checkerboard bands.

In the foreground is F-15B-19-MC 77-0157; in the background are F-15A-19-MC 77-0089 and F-15A-18-MC 77-0082. The "EG" code and blue tail stripes mark these planes as part of the 58th Fighter Squadron, 33rd Fighter Wing, Eglin Air Force Base.

Ground crewmen perform maintenance on an F-15 Eagle assigned to the 18th Tactical Fighter Wing during Exercise Pacific Consort on 19 August 1980. Although a retractable crew ladder was built into the F-15s' fuselages, the detachable ladder seen here was always the preferred means of accessing the cockpit. In the foreground is one of the various ground-support equipment carts that were essential to maintaining the Air Force's jets.

AIM-9 Sidewinder air-to-air missiles on launcher racks on the right-wing pylon of an F-15A are viewed from the front. Yellow safety caps are fitted over the seeker heads of the missiles, and "REMOVE BEFORE FLIGHT" tags are attached to safety pins.

AIM-7F Sparrow air-to-air missiles are mounted on the left side of an F-15 Eagle alert aircraft parked on the flight line at Osan Air Base, Republic of Korea, on 1 October 1980. A close-up view is available of the tail fins and the exhaust of the one in the foreground.

A pilot of the 18th Tactical Fighter Wing is standing up in the cockpit of an F-15 Eagle prior to a mission during Exercise Pacific Consort on 19 August 1980. On the access door of the radar equipment bay is a panel with a black outline in which the armament for the current mission was written with an erasable marker. Visible inside the bay is the array of black boxes associated with the APG-63 pulse-Doppler radar system.

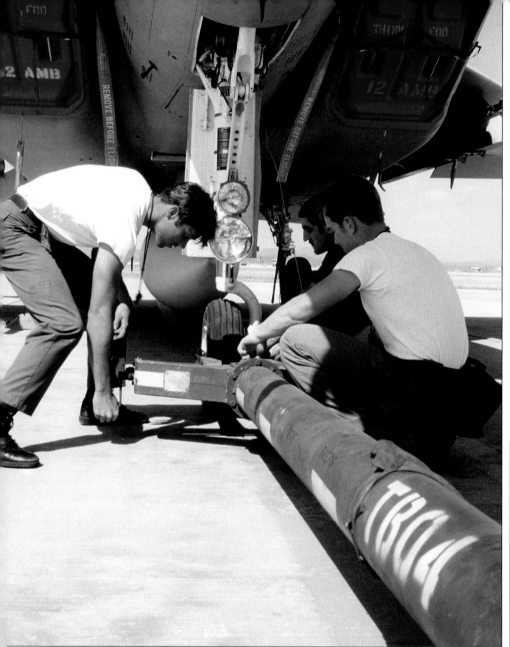

Tech Sgt. Ronald J. Breemen, USAF, is peeling masking tape from the white border of a red hinomaru insignia on an F-15A Eagle that is being prepared for transfer to the Japan Air Self-Defense Force (JASDF) at Kaden Air Force Base, Okinawa, on 24 March 1981.

Senior Airman Carolyn Liddiard gives hand signals to an U.S. Air Force pilot at the controls of an F-15A Eagle destined for the Japan Air Self-Defense Force while taxiing at Kadena Air Base, Okinawa, on 23 April 1981. The JASDF designated its F-15As F-15Js.

Maintenance personnel hook a tow bar to the nose gear of an F-15 Eagle aircraft at Osan Air Base on 1 October 1980. Two light assemblies are on the nose-gear strut: the upper, smaller one is a taxi light. The larger one is the landing light. Red covers are positioned over the engine intakes. Stenciled on them are "12 AMB" and "THINK FOD," a reference to foreign-object damage and a reminder to constantly check the intakes for any debris, no matter how small, which could cause serious damage to the engines.

Two-seat Eagles in the Japanese Air Self-Defense Force are designated F-15DJ. This example, manufactured by Mitsubishi, bore JASDF serial number 92-8068 on the tail, and was assigned to the JASDF's Aggressor Group (Hiko Kyodo-tai) at Nyūtabaru Air Base on the island of Kyūshū, Japan.

Al-Quwwât al-Jawwîyah as-Su'ûdîyah (the Royal Saudi Air Force: RSAF) has acquired numerous F-15s over the decades. This example is an F-15C with tail number 1322. The tail numbers were the Saudis' own, and did not directly correlate to USAF serial numbers. The RSAF insignia was on the side of the engine intake trunk, and the RSAF ensign was on the upper part of the vertical tail.

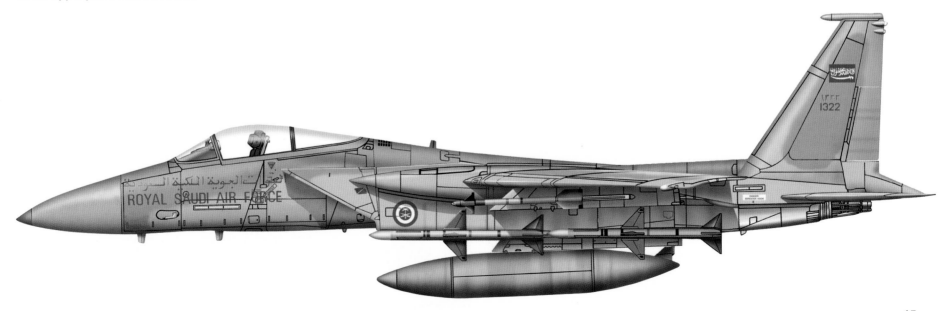

An F-15 banks right out of formation with F-15C-24-MC USAF serial number 79-0019 during a flight in 1981. The "CR" Tail code on the closer plane indicates it was assigned to the 32nd Fighter Squadron. The tail band is orange outlined in green. (National Museum of the United States Air Force)

On a cold, snowy day at Bitburg Air Base, Federal Republic of Germany, on 1 January 1982, an F-15 Eagle is taxiing along the flight line. The aircraft is carrying a 610-gallon centerline auxiliary fuel tank. On the tail is the "CR" code of the 36th Fighter Wing.

A parked F-15 Eagle at an unidentified air base is armed with four AIM-9 Sidewinder air-to-air missiles on 12 June 1981. Aft of the cockpit is the grille for the cockpit air conditioner. The dark areas on the tops of the engine intakes are bleed-air ducts. On the right glove alongside the right engine intake, the two dark squares are ventilation grilles for the M61 20m gun bay; the forward one is an air intake, and the rear one is an air outlet.

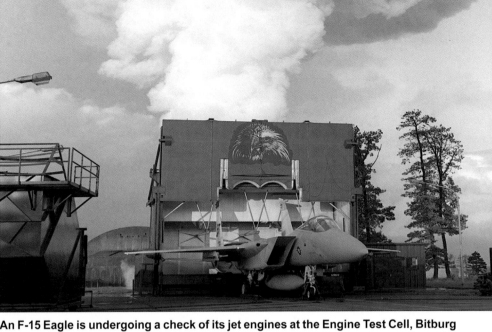

Two F-15s of the 33rd Tactical Fighter Wing, based at Eglin Air Force Base, Florida, are viewed from above during a flight over the water on 28 April 1982. These planes were participating in "Ocean Venture," joint-services maritime war games. (National Museum of the United States Air Force)

An F-15 Eagle is undergoing a check of its jet engines at the Engine Test Cell, Bitburg Air Base, Federal Republic of Germany, on 22 October 1981. Steam is rising from the cell, caused by water being injected into the hot exhaust gases of the engines.

The LTV Aerospace ASM-135 ASAT (Anti-satellite Missile) was designed to be launched by F-15As to knock out enemy satellites. Here, an ASAT is on a bomb-lift truck, with F-15A-18-MC serial number 77-0084 parked in the background, on 1 August 1982. (National Archives)

An F-15C-28-MC, USAF serial number 80-0032, with the "FF" tail code of the 1st Fighter Wing, is undergoing an engine change at a base at Khartoum, Sudan, during Arid Farmer, a deployment made in response to Libyan activities in Chad, on 15 August 1983.

Members of the 12th Aircraft Maintenance Unit install a new Pratt & Whitney F100-PW-100 engine in F-15D-22-MC 78-0566 of the 12th Fighter Squadron, 16th Fighter Wing, during Exercise Cope North 85-1, on 8 November 1984 at Chitose Air Base, Japan.

In a photo taken shortly after the preceding one, technicians from the 12th Aircraft Maintenance Unit have maneuvered a new Pratt & Whitney F100-PW-100 engine partway into the left engine bay of an F-15D during Exercise COPE NORTH 85-1.

An important tactic in modern warfare would be to knock-out enemy reconnaissance and communications satellites. To this end, anti-satellite (ASAT) missiles were developed. An F-15 is seen test-firing one of them near Edwards Air Force Base in September 1985. (National Museum of the United States Air Force)

The lead F-15 of the 1st Tactical Fighter Wing, Langley Air Force Base, Virginia, is seen during a flight on 15 June 1983. "1ST TFW," the tail code "FF," and the Tactical Air Force insignia are on the tail. This eagle is armed with two AIM-9 Sidewinder missiles on the wing pylon and four fuselage-mounted AIM-7 Sparrow missiles. On the engine-intake trunk are the insignias of the three fighter squadrons in the 1st TFW: the 27th TFS, 71st TFS, and 94th TFS.

On 19 March 1986, McDonnell Douglas F-15C-21-MC 78-0489, piloted by Capt. Patrick E. Duffy of the 67th Tactical Fighter Squadron, 18th Tactical Fighter Wing, escorts a Soviet Tupelov TU-95 Bear bomber which had approached the U.S. Fleet during Team Spirit 86, a joint U.S.-South Korean military exercise. The squadron flew numerous escort sorties against intruding Soviet aircraft during the exercise. (National Museum of the United States Air Force)

F-15A-18-MC serial number 77-067, assigned to the 8th Tactical Fighter Squadron, 49th Tactical Fighter Wing, is parked Naval Air Station Whidbey Island in the State of Washington in August 1986. The plane was there to present a flight demonstration. (National Museum of the United States Air Force)

F-15A-17-MC serial number 76-0086, armed with an ASM-135 ASAT missile, is banking to the left over Vandenberg Air Force Base Tracking Station in early 1985. On the vertical tail is an insignia with the legend "ASAT EAGLE" over "SATELLITE KILLER." (National Archives)

A Japan Air Self-Defense Force F-15J pilot awaits the opening of his canopy while parked on a rain-swept flight line at Nyūtabaru Air Base, Japan, during Exercise Cope North 86-4, a joint exercise of Pacific Rim allies, on 11 September 1986.

On 19 March 1987, the first production Strike Eagle, F-15E-41-MC 86-183, foreground, and F-15B-20-MC 77-0166, fly together over Edwards Air Force Base, California. The F-15B has the "ED" tail code of the Air Force Flight Test Center at Edwards AFB. (National Museum of the United States Air Force)

Ground crewmen use a winch and cable to pull a 58th Tactical Fighter Squadron F-15 into its hangar during Exercise Cornet Phaser, a NATO rapid-deployment exercise, at a base at Lahr, Federal Republic of Germany, on 5 October 1987.

F-15C-40-MC 85-0112, of the 33rd Tactical Fighter Wing, fires an AIM-7 Sparrow missile at a target on the Gulf Range as part of Combat Archer, the Weapon System Evaluation Program at Tyndall Air Force Base, Florida, on 1 January 1988.

Its radome and electronics access doors swung open, an F-15 Eagle aircraft is undergoing servicing on a flight line at an unidentified airfield on 30 November 1988. A red cover is fitted over the radar antenna, to protect its delicate and sensitive parts while not in use.

An F-15 is inverted on a pedestal at the Rome Air Development Center's Irish Hill test site near Rome, New York, in July 1986. This was a means of quickly evaluating the effectiveness of a plane's antennas at different angles and with various underwing stores.

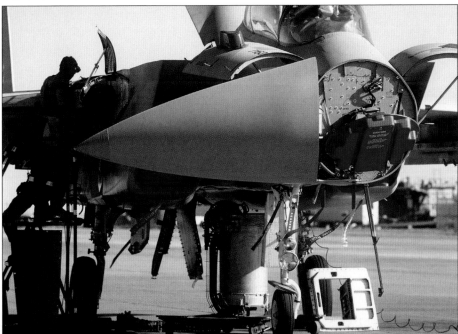

Two F-15E Strike Eagles of the 336th Tactical Fighter Squadron fly in formation in September 1989. The plane in the foreground was crewed by Lt. Cols. M. Decuir and John Delouey, and the one in the background by Capts. Mark Mouw and Gregory Torba. (National Museum of the United States Air Force)

A photographer in a KC-10A tanker took this photo of an F-15E Strike Eagle of the 336th Tactical Fighter Squadron breaking away after being refueled, on 12 September 1989. Visible under the right inlet is the AAQ-13 Navigation Pod of the LANTIRN system. (National Museum of the United States Air Force)

A KC-10 Extender tanker is refueling an F-15E Strike Eagle assigned to the 336th Tactical Fighter Squadron somewhere high over North Carolina on 27 March 1989. Prior to refueling, the door of the refueling receptacle, which was hinged on the front, swung downward into the recess to the front of the receptacle. The door swung back up when refueling was complete. (National Museum of the United States Air Force)

An F-15C of the 33rd Tactical Fighter Wing, based at Eglin Air Force Base, Florida, banks left during a 16 October 1989 flight. It is carrying two AIM-9 Sidewinder missiles on each of the two wing pylons, and four AIM-120 Advanced Medium-Range Air-to-Air Missiles (AMRAAMs) on the fuselage missile stations. A 610-gallon fuel tank is on the centerline. (National Museum of the United States Air Force)

An F-15 Eagle from 49th Tactical Fighter Wing, Holloman AFB, New Mexico, approaches the runway for a landing on or around 1 January 1990. The blue bands on the vertical tail indicate that this plane was serving with the 7th Tactical Fighter Squadron.

Two crewmen from the 58th Operational Support Squadron, 58th Fighter Wing, make last-minute checks of and arm the practice bombs on the pylons of an F-15E Strike Eagle of the 461st Fighter Squadron at Luke Air Force Base, Arizona, on 1 February 1993. (National Museum of the United States Air Force)

NASA operated this HIDEC (Highly Integrated Digital Electronic Control) F-15, seen here while making a landing after a flight out of NASA's Dryden Flight Research Center, Edwards, California, in 1993. Originally, this plane was F-15A USAF serial number 71-0287. It carried NASA aircraft number 835 on the tail. One of the projects it was employed in was the development of a computer-assisted engine-control system that allows a plane to land using only engine power if its control surfaces are disabled.

On 12 April 1993, F-15C-35-MC 84-0019 of the 53rd Fighter Squadron taxis at Aviano Air Base, Italy, before departing on Operation Deny Flight: a mission to enforce a United Nations-sanctioned no-fly zone in Bosnia and Herzegovina. (National Museum of the United States Air Force)

F-15C-37-MC 84-0005 of the 53rd Fighter Squadron is being serviced at Aviano Air Base, Italy, during Operation Deny Flight on 16 April 1993. On the left pylon is the pilot's travel pod, decorated with red and yellow stripes, for carrying his personal gear. (National Museum of the United States Air Force)

A stylized Eagle is on the tail of this F-15A-17-MC, serial number 76-0106, photographed in May 1993 while flying a surveillance mission against drug-runners in Panama. This plane was part of Air Forces Panama, the U.S. Air Force command tasked with the defense of the Panama Canal, and specifically the plane was assigned to Coronet Night Hawk, an all-guard mission that employed both F-15s and F-16s on a 24-hour-alert basis. (National Museum of the United States Air Force)

In June 1994, F-15C-37-MC 84-0014, assigned to the 53rd Fighter Squadron, 36th Fighter Wing, has landed at Aviano Air Base, Italy, for maintenance following a combat mission over Bosnia to enforce the no-fly zone. The 53rd FS's yellow band is at the top of the tail. (National Museum of the United States Air Force)

F-15D-40-MC 85-0134 of the 33rd Fighter Wing prepares to taxi to the runway at Roosevelt Roads Naval Air Station, Puerto Rico, around 1 September 1994. It was part of a flight of 24 F-15s on a return trip to their home base at Eglin Air Force Base, Florida.

The Israeli Air Force operated this F-15C, tail number 840. It is shown during its service with 106 Squadron. During its career, this Eagle was credited with shooting down six Syrian planes; six kill markings are on the fuselage forward of the windscreen, below which is repeated the tail number, 840. The inscription on the radome translates to "Skyblazer."

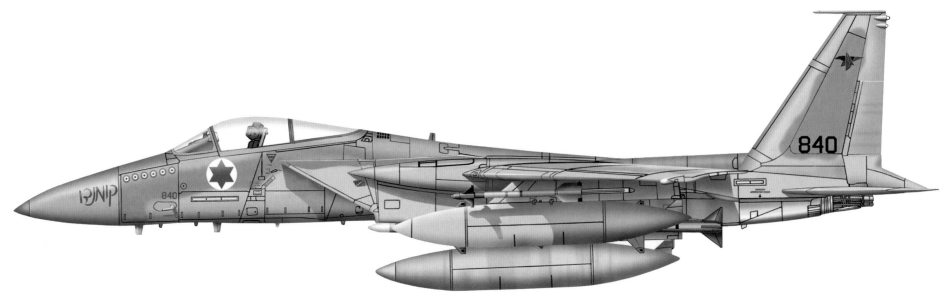

The first preproduction TF-15A (F-15B), 71-0290, was converted to the colorfully painted F-15 STOL/MTD (Short Takeoff and Landing/Maneuver Technology Demonstrator) while on loan to NASA in the 1980s. When this photo was taken around early 1996, the plane was being used as the F-15 ACTIVE (Advanced Control Technology for Integrated Vehicles), a joint project of NASA, the U.S. Air Force, McDonnell Douglas Aerospace, and Pratt & Whitney, from 1993 to 1999. The plane was powered by Pratt & Whitney F100-PW-229 engines modified with multidirectional thrust vectoring nozzles. On 24 April 1996 this aircraft completed its first supersonic yaw vectoring flight at Dryden Flight Research Center, Edwards, California.

A new Pratt & Whitney F100-PW-220E turbofan engine for an F-15 Eagle, a power plant designed to reduce maintenance hours, is being operated in the test-cell hush house (a chamber used to reduce noise pollution) at Kadena Air Base, Japan, on 11 May 1998.

On 6 November 2001, F-15A-19-MC 77-0102 of the 102nd Fighter Wing, Massachusetts Air National Guard, flies a combat air patrol (CAP) mission over New York City during Operation Noble Eagle, a homeland security operation in the wake of 9/11.

A USAF maintenance technician is standing inside the left engine bay of an F-15 Eagle during a major overhaul of the aircraft around 1999, shining a red flashlight on the interior of the compartment while he inspects it. Another maintenance tech, crouching at the lower left of the photo, jots down any discrepancies in the aircraft-maintenance forms.

In May 2002 an F-15A-20-MC, USAF serial number 77-0134, assigned to the 122nd Fighter Squadron, Louisiana Air National Guard, based at New Orleans, cruises over Cape San Blas, Florida. The plane and crew had just completed a Combat Archer training mission. Combat Archer, also known as the Air-to-Air Weapons-Evaluation Program, was hosted by the 83rd Fighter Weapons Squadron at Tyndall Air Force Base, Florida. The tail band is purple, yellow, and green, with five fleur-de-lis on the yellow part; "Louisiana" is written above the band. The "JZ" tail code stands for, of course, "Jazz." (National Museum of the United States Air Force)

An F-15E of the 332nd Air Expeditionary Group is departing on a bombing mission to Afghanistan on 7 November 2001. It is armed with a GBU-15 electro-optic guided bomb under the right wing, its associated AN-AXQ-14 data link pod under the fuselage centerline, and a GBU-12 Paveway II laser-guided bomb on the right CFT.

F-15A-19-MC serial number 77-0118 with "SL" markings for the 131st Fighter Wing prepares to take off from Prince Sultan Air Base, Saudi Arabia, during Operation Southern Watch on 24 October 2000. This operation was to enforce a mandated no-fly/no-drive zone in southern Iraq. (National Archives)

McDonnell Douglas F-15E-58-MC Strike Eagle USAF serial number 96-0205, serving with 492 48th Fighter Wing, based at RAF Lakenheath, England, catches a Mobile Aircraft Arresting System (MAAS) wire during a deployment to Ṭallîl Air Base, near an-Nâṣirîyah, in southern Iraq, in support of Operation Iraqi Freedom on 25 May 2004. The tail code is LN, and the tail bands are blue with white borders.

Ground crewmen remove the MAAS cable from the arrestor hook of the same F-15E depicted in the preceding photo, after landing at Ṭallîl Air Base. A tow bar is secured to the nose landing gear, to enable a tractor to pull the aircraft to its parking area.

This long view of the same F-15E seen in the two preceding photos shows more of the MAAS cable, which is still attached to the arrestor hook. The rear ends of the cable are attached to tires, which in turn are fastened to thick webbing straps.

F-15C-23-MCs of the 44th Fighter Squadron, 18th Fighter Wing, based at Kadena Air Base, Japan, fly in formation over Okinawa on 4 May 2004. On the pylons are AIM-120 AMRAAMs and Combat Training System/Tactical Combat Training System pods. Activated on 1 January 1944, the 44th Fighter Squadron served with distinction in the South Pacific and Southwest Pacific in World War II, and flew missions against North Vietnam from bases in Thailand during the Vietnam War. The 44th Fighter Squadron was based at Kadena Air Base from March 1971 on, with occasional deployments to a variety of bases in the Western Pacific. The squadron first acquired the F-15Cs in February 1980, flying that model of the Eagle for many years thereafter.

This extreme close-up view of the aerial refueling of an F-15E Strike Eagle of the 335th Fighter Squadron, 4th Fighter Wing, based at Seymour Johnson Air Force Base, North Carolina, was taken by a photographer in a KC-10A Extender cargo/tanker of the 763rd Expeditionary Air Refueling Squadron, Al Dhafra Air Base, United Arab Emirates, during a combat mission in support of Operation Iraqi Freedom on 16 August 2004. The Strike Eagle is armed with AIM-120A AMRAAMs on the outboard side of the pylons and AIM-9M Sidewinders on the inboard sides of the pylons. Four GBU-12 500-pound bombs are visible under the CFT, and the front end of an AN/AAQ-28(V) targeting pod can be seen under the left engine intake.

Two Israeli Defense Forces/Air Force F-15I Eagles practice air-defense maneuvers during a training mission over the Nevada Test and Training Ranges at Nellis Air Force Base, Nevada, during Exercise Red Flag in 2004. Exercise Red Flag is a realistic combat-training exercise in which the air forces of the United States and its allies hone their crafts. The IDF/AF became interested in acquiring the F-15 Eagle by 1974, when its pilots tested the TF-15A. The following year, Israel submitted an order for 25 F-15As. Deliveries of F-15s to Israel commenced in December 1976. Israeli F-15s first drew blood in 1979, and subsequently they have been credited with shooting down many Syrian fighter planes, and they have conducted numerous long-range missions, such as the raid on Palestine Liberation Organization headquarters in Tunis, Tunisia, on 1 October 1985.

Using a special ammo cart, armorers of the 123rd Fighter Squadron, 142nd Fighter Wing, Oregon National Guard, load 20mm ammunition into an F-15 Eagle during the William Tell 2004 gunnery competition at Tyndall Air Force Base, Florida, on 10 November 2004.

Staff Sgt. Kevin Skaggs of the 95th Air Maintenance Unit wrestles a flex chute into place, to send 940 rounds of 20mm training projectiles into an F-15 Eagle during a flight-line loading competition at William Tell 2004, Tyndall Air Force Base, on 12 November 2004.

During the Hawaii Air National Guard Operational Readiness Exercise at Hickam Air Force Base, Hawaii, in February 2004, an aircraft maintainer wearing Mission Oriented Protective Posture level-4 (MOPP-4) gear checks the left rudder of F-15A-18-MC USAF serial number 76-0120. This Eagle was assigned to the 154th Wing, based at Hickam Air Force Base. A clear view is available of, from top to bottom on the trailing edge of the left tail, the AN/ALQ-128 Electronic Warfare Warning system antenna, the AN/ALR-56 Radar Warning Receiver antenna, and the red anti-collision light. At the top of the right tail is a spike-shaped harmonic balancer, and on the rear of that tail are an AN/ALR-56 antenna and red anti-collision light.

McDonnell Douglas F-15C-35-MC serial number 83-0027 from the 27th Tactical Fighter Squadron flies past the Pyramids of Giza during a deployment to the Middle East. The squadron insignia, featuring an eagle over a red disk on a yellow circular background, is on the engine intake. (National Archives)

The tanker refueling this F-15E Strike Eagle during April 2006 has cast a shadow across the cockpit area. Three AIM-120 AMRAAMs are visible on the launcher rack. The fronts of two laser-guided bombs can be seen under the right conformal fuel tank.

F-15E-42-MC 86-0189 of the 335th Fighter Squadron (indicated by the green bands at the tops of the vertical tails), 4th Fighter Wing, is parked at an unidentified base. The insignia of the 4th Fighter Wing is on the front of the CFT.

The right vertical tail of F-15A-19-MC 77-0098 is shown. This plane, the last F-15 to be retired from the Oregon Air National Guard, served with the 123rd Fighter Squadron "Redhawks," 142nd Fighter Wing, at Portland International Airport.

Two F-15 Eagles with "aggressor" camouflage schemes accompany a USAF F-22 Raptor fighter during a training mission over Nevada on 24 April 2008. The Eagles were assigned to the 65th Aggressor Squadron at Nellis Air Force Base. In the tan and brown camouflage in the foreground is F-15D-39-MC 85-0129, while the blue-on-blue plane appears to be F-15C-27-MC 80-0018.

Photographed in January 2009, this modified F-15B, NASA tail number 836, has served as a supersonic research testbed and mission-support aircraft for NASA's Armstrong Flight Research Center in Edwards, California, since the early 1990s.

Afterburners glowing, NASA's NF-15B soars from the runway at Edwards Air Force Base on its final flight. Test pilot Jim Smolka was as the controls. The first two-seat F-15, it had a useful career as a test plane for McDonnell Douglas, the Air Force, and NASA.

NASA's canard-equipped NF-15B research plane, tail number 837, takes off from Edwards Air Force Base on its last flight on 30 January 2009. The canards of the NF-15B had a span of 26.5 feet, compared with the plane's wingspan of 42.8 feet.

NASA Dryden's NF-15B, tail number 837, is parked on a hardstand, canards tilted down, during a pre-flight control check prior to a Lancets (Lift and Nozzle Change Effects on Tail ShockProject) flight, part of a project to design quieter supersonic aircraft.

F-15C-23-MC 78-0528 of the 65th Aggressor Squadron flies over Nevada on 17 May 2012. This plane and others in its squadron flew in support of, and engaged in simulated dogfights against, members of the Air Force Weapons School at Nellis, a five-and-a-half-month training course that provides advanced training in weapons and tactics employment.

McDonnell Douglas F-15E serial number 88-1708, from the 4th Fighter Wing, permanently based at Seymour Johnson Air Force Base, North Carolina, has just taken off on a mission from Bagrâm Air Field, Afghanistan, on 15 December 2011. (Tech. Sgt. Matt Hecht / U.S. Air National Guard)

F-15D-27-MC 80-0054 of the 57th Fighter Wing at Nellis Air Force Base, Nevada, has a distinguished passenger aboard. The crew placard, decorated with an eagle head, alongside the cockpit lists pilot Maj. Julius Romasanta and Gen. Chuck Yeager.

A Japan Air Self-Defense Force F-15 Eagle, tail number 82-8965, takes off from Eileson Air Force Base, Alaska, during Red Flag-Alaska 13-3 on 9 August 2013. An insignia constituting a yellow eagle inside a black circlular background is on the vertical tail.

The same JASDF F-15 Eagle shown in the preceding photo is viewed from a slightly different perspective during takeoff from Eileson Air Force Base. The Japanese sent six aircraft and more than 150 airmen to participate in Red Flag-Alaska 13-3.

An F-15E Strike Eagle of the 391st Fighter Squadron is releasing defensive flares during a close-air-support mission during exercise Mountain Roundup 2013, at Saylor Creek bombing range near Mountain Home Air Force Base, Idaho, on 16 October 16 2013.

One of the last three F-15 Eagle fighter aircraft assigned to the 120th Fighter Wing takes off from the Great Falls, Montana, International Airport on 24 October 2013. Those Eagles were transferred to the California Air National Guard on that date.

On 26 November 2013 an Israeli Defense Forces/Air Force F-15D takes off from Uvda Air Force Base, Israel, during Blue Flag: a multinational aerial-warfare exercise hosted by Israel to foster greater coordination between the air forces of the U.S., Israel, Greece, and Italy.

An F-15C-35-MC, 84-0014, assigned to Col. Clay Garrison but piloted by Col. John York, 144th Fighter Wing Operations Group Commander, flies over Central California on 7 November 2013. The wing was transitioning to the F-15 from the F-16.

Personnel of the 48th Aircraft Maintenance Squadron perform post-flight servicing on an F-15E Strike Eagle in preparation for the Blue Flag exercise at Uvda Air Force Base, Israel, on 19 November 2013. The insignia of the 492nd Fighter Squadron is on the CFT.

A column of F-15E Strike Eagles of the 492nd Fighter Squadron, based at Royal Air Force Lakenheath, taxis at Uvda Air Force Base, Israel, after a simulated combat mission during the Blue Flag exercise on 26 November 2013.

An F-15E Strike Eagle takes off from Uvda Air Force Base, Israel, during Blue Flag on 27 November 2013. On the vertical tail are the "LN" tail code of the 48th Fighter Wing and the blue tail band, with white edging, of the 492nd Fighter Squadron.

Two U.S. Air Force F-15E Strike Eagles fly in formation over northern Iraq around dawn on 23 September 2014, after conducting airstrikes in Syria. These aircraft were part of a large coalition strike force that was the first to attack targets in Syria of the terror organization that called itself "the Islamic State in Iraq and the Levant" (ISIL) (also called "Islamic State in Iraq and Syria" [ISIS] or referred to by the Arabic acronym "Daesh" or "Dâ'ish," derived from the group's Arabic name: *ad-Dawlah al-Islâmîyah fî al-'Irâq wa-ash-Shâm*).

Speed brake deployed, an F-15E with the 428th Fighter Squadron lands at Luke Air Force Base, Arizona, on 19 November 2015, during the training exercise Forging Sabre, a joint exercise with Republic of Singapore armed forces. Singapore and U.S. flags are painted on the tail for the occasion. (Senior Airman James Hensley / U.S. Air Force)

A F-15C of the 144th Fighter Wing from Fresno, California, prepares to depart from the Canadian Forces Base Goose Bay in Labrador, Canada, on a mission on 22 October 2015 during Vigilant Shield 16. The exercise was held in Newfoundland and Labrador.

F-15E 98-0134 of the 492nd Fighter Squadron, 48th Fighter Wing, prepares to depart RAF Lakenheath to support Operation Inherent Resolve, 12 November 2015. The wing was deploying six F-15Es to Incirlik Air Base, Turkey, to conduct counter-ISIL missions.

The pilot and the WSO of an F-15E Strike Eagle of the 48th Fighter Wing wait expectantly for clearance to take off from RAF Lakenheath, bound for Incirlik Air Base, to support Operation Inherent Resolve, 12 November 2015.

An F-15E Strike Eagle of the 48th Fighter Wing (the "Statue of Liberty Wing") lands at Incirlik Air Base, Turkey, on 12 November 2015. Among the under-wing stores are AIM-120 AMRAAMs and two travel pods. (Note: The two travel pods are mounted on the CFTs, although it does appear that the rear one is mounted below the right drop tank.)

A crewman from the 494th Fighter Squadron exits from his F-15 while the other crewman stands on the fuselage, upon arriving at Incirlik Air Base on 12 November 2015. The insignia of the 494th Fighter Squadron is on the front of the CFT.

As darkness approaches, a column of three F-15Es taxis behind a follow-me car after landing at Incirlik Air Base on 12 November 2015. Soon, these Strike Eagles would be flying all-weather strike missions against ISIL forces in both Iraq and Syria.

Boeing F-15E-62-MC Strike Eagle serial number 98-0131, with the 48th Fighter Wing, is preparing for takeoff from RAF Lakenheath, bound for Incirlik Air Base, Turkey, from where it will conduct missions against ISIL in Iraq and Syria under Operation Inherent Resolve, on 12 November 2015. (Senior Airman Erin Trower / USAF)

F-15C-38-MC 84-0017, assigned to the 144th Fighter Wing, prepares for takeoff at the Fresno Air National Guard Base on 22 January 2016. This plane was part of eight F-15s bound for Nellis Air Force Base to participate in the Red Flag 16-01 exercise.

After a crack was discovered in the wing of F-15C-21-MC 78-0482, assigned to the 142nd Fighter Wing, Portland, Oregon, the Depot Field Team from the 402nd Aircraft Maintenance Group, Robins Air Force Base, Georgia, is removing the old wings on 6 December 2016, preparatory to installing new ones. (U.S. Air National Guard photo by Senior Master Sgt. Shelly Davison, 142nd Fighter Wing Public Affairs)

In a companion view to the preceding photo, the Depot Field Team, 402nd Aircraft Maintenance Group, has separated the left wing from the fuselage of the F-15C. With the wing removed, details of the interior of the wing-root area are available, including plumbing and the wing-attachment lugs. (U.S. Air National Guard photo by Senior Master Sgt. Shelly Davison, 142nd Fighter Wing Public Affairs)

A 67th Fighter Squadron F-15C returns to Kadena Air Base, Japan, after a flight on 29 July 2016. This plane had logged 10,000 flight hours, making it the first F-15 based at Kadena to achieve that distinction. The 18th Fighter Wing's "ZZ" code is on the tail.

An F-15C assigned to the 194th Expeditionary Fighter Squadron, California Air National Guard, buzzes the flightline during an air show at Campia Turzii, Romania, 23 July 2016, during the squadron's six-month deployment to Europe in support of NATO.

On 24 August 2016, F-15C-35-MC 83-0012 of the 122nd Fighter Squadron, 159th Fighter Wing, prepares for takeoff at Nellis Air Force Base during Red Flag 16-4. These were practice exercises to accustom crews to highly contested combat environments.

A Massachusetts Air National Guard F-15C of the 104th Fighter Wing comes in for a landing at Graf Ignatievo, Bulgaria, 8 September 2016. It was part of a force of four F-15Cs sent to assist the Bulgarian Air Force to police the host nation's sovereign airspace.

F-15E-46-MC 88-1707 flies over Iraq on 29 November 2016 carrying a mixed load of JDAMs, GBUs, and air-to-air missiles in the war against ISIL. This plane is assigned to the 366th Operations Group, based at Mountain Home Air Force Base, Idaho.

This F-15A at Davis-Monthan Air Force Base, Arizona, in November 2015 is being prepared for static display at the Western Air Defense Sector Air Park at Joint Base Lewis-McChord, Washington. It was installed at its new home in June 2016.

A MiG 29 Fulcrum of the Bulgarian Air Force is in the foreground, and several F-15C Eagles are in the background, in a photo taken during a visit by the 122nd Expeditionary Fighter Squadron to Graf Ignatievo Air Base, Bulgaria, in support of Operation Atlantic Resolve in late April 2017. (U.S. Air Force photo by Tech. Sgt. Staci Miller)

The right engine has been removed from an F-15C during Exercise Northern Edge 17 at Joint Base Elmendorf-Richardson in Alaska on 4 May 2017. The engine, which was burning excessive oil, was pulled from the plane and replaced with another engine in under three hours.

While making a hard banking maneuver, a USAF F-15E Strike Eagle is firing flares during a mission for Operation Inherent Resolve, the campaign against ISIL, on 21 June 2017. The aircraft is carrying a load of six 500-pound GBU-38/B JDAMs under each FAST conformal fuel tank. (U.S. Air Force photo by Staff Sgt. Trevor T. McBride)

McDonnell Douglas F-15E-51-MC Strike Eagle serial number 91-316, from the 492nd Expeditionary Fighter Squadron, is being prepared for takeoff next to a hardened hangar at a base in Southwest Asia on 9 October 2017. In the background, an F-16 Falcon is taking off on a mission.

An F-15E Strike Eagle, serial number 91-605, from the 492nd Fighter Squadron is taking off on a training sortie at Royal Air Force Lakenheath, England, on 6 November 2017. At the time, this squadron had recently returned from a deployment to Southwest Asia. (U.S. Air Force photo/Staff Sgt. Emerson Nuñez)

An airman from the 48th Component Maintenance Squadron uses a penlight to inspect a Pratt & Whitney F100-PW-229 engine in a shop at Royal Air Force Lakenheath, England, on 12 December 2017. The engine is from an F-15E of the 48th Fighter Wing. (U.S. Air Force photo/Tech. Sgt. Emerson Nuñez)

Personnel from the 173rd Fighter Wing and 550th Fighter Squadron and their families greet Santa Claus as he disembarks from an F-15D during the wing's annual children's Christmas party at Kingsley Field, Oregon, on 3 December 2017. (U.S. Air National Guard photo by Staff Sgt. Penny Snoozy)

A U.S. Air Force F-15E Strike Eagle rests on its hardstand shortly after landing at İncirlik Air Base, Turkey, on 12 November 2015 during a support mission for military operations against ISIL in Iraq and Syria. Although the sun is setting on this particular plane, the F-15 Eagles, now with over four decades of stellar service behind them, will continue to serve the United States in years to come